AF408257

Mueller Austria Juicer Recipe Book

The Complete Home-made Tasty Juicing Recipes Book for Your Whole Family

By Jenny Alisa

© Copyright 2020 -Jenny Alisa - All rights reserved.

In no way is it legal to reproduce, duplicate, or transmit any part of this document by either electronic means or in printed format. Recording of this publication is strictly prohibited, and any storage of this material is not allowed unless with written permission from the publisher. All rights reserved.
The information provided herein is stated to be truthful and consistent, in that any liability, regarding inattention or otherwise, by any usage or abuse of any policies, processes, or directions contained within is the solitary and complete responsibility of the recipient reader. Under no circumstances will any legal liability or blame be held against the publisher for any reparation, damages, or monetary loss due to the information herein, either directly or indirectly. Respective authors own all copyrights not held by the publisher.

Legal Notice:
This book is copyright protected. This is only for personal use. You cannot amend, distribute, sell, use, quote or paraphrase any part or the content within this book without the consent of the author or copyright owner. Legal action will be pursued if this is breached.

Disclaimer Notice:
Please note the information contained within this document is for educational and entertainment purposes only. Every attempt has been made to provide accurate, up to date and reliable, complete information. No warranties of any kind are expressed or implied. Readers acknowledge that the author is not engaging in the rendering of legal, financial, medical or professional advice.

By reading this document, the reader agrees that under no circumstances are we responsible for any losses, direct or indirect, which are incurred as a result of the use of information contained within this document, including, but not limited to, —errors, omissions, or inaccuracies.

Table of Contents

Introduction

A large number of the population suffers from various diseases due to poor diet.

The rise of fast food and highly processed products in the market has made a generation deficient in the essential nutrients from fresh fruits and vegetables.

Apart from integrating more fresh food into our diet, which is the apparent course of action, there are individuals who just find this hard to do.

Juicing enables people who do not like to eat fruits and vegetables to consume and enjoy its health benefits.

It is also an excellent way to introduce vegetables to children's diets and have them get accustomed to the taste.

Juicing has endured other health trends over the years due to the many people attesting to a myriad of health benefits including glowing skin, improved energy, better digestion, and weight loss.

It's about time you make the most of its benefits too.

Chapter 1: Mueller Austria Juicer 101

A juicer or sometimes referred to as juice extractor is a device used to draw out the liquids from fruits and vegetables.

It immediately separates the pulp leaving you with a pure extract that is ready to drink. Usually, vegetables and fruits are combined in order to get the maximum nutritional benefits.

A good juicer should be powerful enough to handle both soft and hard produce.

Mueller Austria is a manufacturer of a broad range of home and kitchen appliances like peelers, electric coffee grinders, electric kettles, rice cookers, and oven toasters.

Its juice extractor is among consumer's top-rated favorites because it is easy to operate, looks premium, and gives them the best value for money among many similar juicers in the market.

What is the Mueller Austria Juicer?

The Mueller Austria juicer is a powerful yet affordable centrifugal juicer that can handle various fruits and vegetables.

The components such as the pulp extractor, lid, plunger, filter bowl, and jug are all made of durable, BPA-free plastic that is easy to clean and maintain.

It offers a generous 3-inch chute that will let you juice whole apples and similar produce with no difficulty. It also features a safety lock that will keep the lid securely covered while the juicer is in use.

The main body is made with stainless steel that looks elegant and will stand out in your kitchen counter. Its heavy-duty stainless steel blade coupled with a robust motor is capable of up to 18,000 revolutions per minute.

This guarantees that the juicer is well capable of handling most of the produce you wish to juice. Around the blade, you will find a fine mesh filter made of food-safe stainless steel that will prevent pulp from clogging the device or getting into your juice.

Underneath the juicer, you will find silicone suction cups that hold it in place. All the parts are easy to assemble and disassemble within seconds. Clean up is made easier since the unit comes with a plastic cleaning brush. These detachable parts are also dishwasher safe.

Mueller Austria's centrifugal juicer has an 1100-watt motor and a two-speed setting to accommodate a wider range of produce. As an added safety feature, the juicer will automatically shut off if the motor overheats. With this much power, you will be able to juice about 16 ounces in eight seconds only.

How Does it Work?

To start juicing, place your choice of vegetable and fruit on the chute and turn on the juicer.

The high-speed motor will cause the blade to rotate and rapidly shred these to bits while the extract passes through the micro mesh and onto the juice jug that can hold about 16 ounces.

Use the plunger to push the produce further into the blades. The pulp will eventually collect and fall into the pulp collector that can hold about 68 ounces.

Use the slow speed setting marked ‘1’ for softer produce such as tomatoes, strawberries, kiwis, and oranges. The faster setting marked ‘2’ is more suitable for tougher produce such as carrots, cucumbers, apples, celery, and kale.

Steps to Getting Started with Using this Juicer

If you have not tried juicing before, it will be helpful to look for recipes online to get you started.

Juicing is fairly easy, and there are no strict rules. You can start combining fruits and vegetables you already like to get used to it. You can gradually add more vegetables to get more nutrients and enzymes from your juice.

If you have any existing health conditions, it is best to consult your nutritionist or general health practitioner first. Diabetics should limit the fruits in their juices as it contains high amounts of sugar.

They can still enjoy the benefits of juicing by loading up on ingredients that are proven to stabilize blood sugar levels like leafy greens such as kale, spinach, celery, and broccoli. You may also pair these with cucumbers, tomatoes, avocados, garlic, ginger, lemon, or lime.

Chapter 2: Tips for Successful and Convenient Juicing

If you are among the many people who have been meaning to try out juicing for its health benefits, here are some useful tips to you can follow to make it worthwhile.

- Consume the juice immediately – Raw-juiced vegetables are packed with lots of nutrients, but it naturally degrades over time. To get the most of the essential vitamins and minerals, drink the juice within a few minutes of juicing. If you need to take it later in the day, you may store the juice in a glass container that is airtight. If possible, fill it to the brim to prevent oxygen from getting in contact as this causes the juice to oxidize and lose phytonutrients.

- Improvise – One great thing about juicing is that you can make your very own recipes. You can combine fruits and vegetables to match your dietary requirements. Moreover, you will be able to consume vegetables you do not normally like by mixing them with others that you already do.
- Check for organic suppliers in your area – Since you are juicing raw produce, it is important to pick only organic. If you are planning to include juices to your regular diet permanently, growing your own vegetables is a viable option to avoid harmful pesticides from commercially grown produce.
- Wash your produce thoroughly – Since we are using raw vegetables, it is paramount to wash our vegetables carefully to remove impurities. If you do not have access to organic products, you may soak commercial produce in four parts water and one part vinegar for at least 20 minutes before rinsing them with running water.
- Replace your coffee with green juice in the morning – Drinking green juice is a great alternative if you want to reduce your caffeine or sugar intake.
- Spice it up – Juicing green vegetables can sometimes be too bitter or boring for some. Adding a lime, lemon, ginger, or spices at the end can help improve the flavor. You can also add mint leaves and other herbs to more dimension to the taste.
- Clean the juicer immediately after use – Letting the pulp sit for a few hours will make clean up harder. Rinse the detachable components right after using, and you will find it almost effortless to wash.
- Put a plastic bag or compostable produce bag over the pulp collector – This also makes clean up easier since all you need to do after is remove the bag and rinse the collector.

Chapter 3: FAQs

1. What are the health benefits of juicing?

Juicing can be highly beneficial for people wanting to lose weight or increase their intake of fruits and vegetables. Consuming fresh vegetables that have cancer-fighting properties will decrease the likelihood of developing a range of illnesses.

A glass of freshly juiced produce is loaded with nutrients to help recharge your immune defense.

It also packs enzymes that promote the creation of good bacteria in the gut. 99% of the microbes in our body can be found in the gut and is responsible for the proper balance and functioning of our central nervous system.

A healthy balance of good and bad bacteria in your microbiome will help fight off infections, promote brain functions, and improve heart health.

2. Can juicing make you lose weight?

It depends on how you will incorporate juicing in your regular diet. Some people find it helpful to undergo juice cleanses for a few days, as it is believed to flush out toxins from the body.

A juice cleanse will help you lose weight since it will require you to stop consuming highly processed foods, caffeine, and dairy. In the same sense, if you watch what you eat and increase your intake of fruits and vegetables through juicing, you will be able to see results down the line.

Having said that, it is important to stress that juicing alone will not be sufficient in providing all the necessary vitamins our body needs. When you go on a juice cleanse, make sure that you have an adequate intake of dietary fiber since this is lost when you consume only the juice of the fruit or vegetable.

3. Is juicing safe for diabetics?

It is better to consult with your nutritionist first if you have diabetes. Fruit juice is high in sugar and can cause blood sugar levels to spike. You may opt for the 80:20 ratio of vegetables to fruits to keep glucose levels under control.

4. Can I juice a big batch to drink for later?

It is best to use just the right amount of produce that you can drink immediately in order to preserve the vitamins and minerals. But if this is not possible, you may store the juices in airtight glass containers inside the refrigerator.

5. Should I only use organic produce?

Ideally, yes. Juicing raw produce that has chemicals and pesticides will mean more harm than help. Look for organic farmers in your area or consider growing a vegetable garden to ensure that you are not putting any harmful substances in your food.

6. Do I need to add water to my juice?

You do not need to add any water when using a juicer. Fruits and vegetables have natural water content to produce juice by themselves. But you can also add water to the juice extracted if you want your juice to have thinner consistency.

7. How does it taste?

Like most things, it will take some getting used to. Green juice or the extract you get from juicing green vegetables taste bitter by themselves. Not everyone will appreciate the taste on their first try. Mixing some fruits can enhance the flavor.

One way to help you get through that is by considering your reasons why you are juicing in the first place. If you are doing it to improve your health, you will find it easier to acknowledge that it's not supposed to taste good all the time. The more you experiment with recipes, the more you'll find the right mixture of ingredients that will suit your taste buds.

8. What do I do with all the pulp?

If you're someone who feels bad for tossing heaps of fresh pulp to the garbage, don't worry because there are a bunch of ways you can reuse it.

There are recipes available online on how to cook muffins, crackers, and veggie burgers, among others. You can also gather and freeze them to make or add to your broths and soups in the future.

Fruit and vegetable pulp can be added to your smoothie, baked goodies, dips, and even scrambled eggs. If you end up with so much, then you can always use it as a compost material.

9. Why buy a juicer if I can buy from juice bars?

When you juice fresh produce with a juicer, the extract is fresher and has no preservatives. You will be able to drink it instantly and enjoy more vitamins, minerals, enzymes, and rich flavonoids.

Store-bought versions can be more expensive and may contain added sugars. Some might even have undergone processing that will extend its shelf life but will also reduce the nutrient content.

10. Is the juice from a juicer different from a smoothie?

Yes. The main difference is that when you use a juice extractor, the pulp is separated, and you will be left with just the liquid extract. A smoothie is made with a high-speed blender and includes the fibers and membranes of the plant.
Juices are usually consumed if you want to detox or cleanse. Smoothies are great if you want to lose weight since the fiber in the pulp leaves you fuller for longer.

Chapter 4: 80 Recipes

Juices for Health

Anti-Inflammatory Juice

Serves: 2
Preparation and Cooking Time: 5 minutes

Ingredients:

4 stalks celery
1 cucumber
1 cup pineapple chunks
1 cup spinach, chopped
1/2 green apple
1 ginger
1 lemon

Preparation:

1) Add celery and cucumber to your Mueller Austria juicer.
2) Process the remaining ingredients.
3) Mix well.
4) Consume immediately.

Serving Suggestion: Garnish with pineapple slice.

Tip: You can use either fresh pineapple or canned pineapple chunks

Energy Boosting Juice

Serves: 4
Preparation and Cooking Time: 10 minutes

Ingredients:

1 orange
3 carrots
1 banana
2 kale leaves
2 cups cold water

Preparation:

1) Process the orange in your Mueller Austria juicer.
2) Add orange juice to serving glasses.
3) Repeat steps for the rest of the ingredients.
4) Add to the serving glasses.
5) Stir in cold water.

Serving Suggestion: Garnish with orange slices.

Tip: Use ripe banana for this recipe.

Detox Juice

Serves: 1-2
Preparation and Cooking Time: 5 minutes

Ingredients:

1 head celery
1 teaspoon turmeric powder
1 teaspoon ground ginger

Preparation:

1) Slice the celery into smaller pieces.
2) Run through your Mueller Austria juicer.
3) Add juice to a serving glass.
4) Stir in turmeric powder and ground ginger.

Serving Suggestion: Sprinkle with a little bit of turmeric powder on top before serving.

Tip: Add sugar to sweeten the taste.

Sweet Detox Juice

Serves: 2
Preparation and Cooking Time: 15 minutes

Ingredients:

2 cups baby spinach
1 cup parsley
1 green apple
1 cucumber
1 lemon

Preparation:

1) Peel the apple and remove the core.
2) Chop the apple.
3) Slice the ginger and cucumber in half.
4) Press these through the Mueller Austria juicer.
5) Mix well.

Serving Suggestion: Serve with ice.

Tip: If the juice is too tart, add 1 carrot.

Liver Cleansing Juice

Serves: 4
Preparation and Cooking Time: 10 minutes

Ingredients:

1 apple
2 beets
2 carrots
2 cups blueberries
1 ginger
1 lemon
1/2 cup broccoli
1 cup coconut water

Preparation:

1) Chop all the ingredients.
2) Feed the ingredients through your Mueller Austria juicer.
3) Pour in coconut water.
4) Process all the ingredients.

Serving Suggestion: Serve with ice.

Tip: It's better to use pure coconut water for this recipe.

Energizing Juice

Serves: 1
Preparation and Cooking Time: 20 minutes

Ingredients:

1 to 2 beets
3 carrots
2 apples
1/2 cucumber
1 tablespoon ginger, minced

Preparation:

1) Process beets in the Mueller Austria juicer, followed by carrots, and then the rest of the ingredients.
2) Chill for a few minutes before serving.

Serving Suggestion: Sprinkle with powdered sugar before serving.

Tip: Use 1 large beet or 2 medium beets. Chop the vegetables into smaller pieces to fit the

Antioxidant Juice

Serves: 2
Preparation and Cooking Time: 5 minutes

Ingredients:

2 beets
1 cup strawberries
1 cup blueberries

Preparation:

1) Slice beets into wedges.
2) Slice strawberries and blueberries in half.
3) Process all ingredients in your Mueller Austria juicer.
4) Serve cold or in room temperature.

Serving Suggestion: Sprinkle with chopped mint leaves.

Tip: You can add more berries to this recipe if you like such as raspberries and blackberries.

Beautifying Juice

Serves: 2
Preparation and Cooking Time: 15 minutes

Ingredients:

3 carrots
2 beets
1 apple
1 lemon
1 cup kale leaves, sliced
4 celery stalks
1 ginger, chopped

Preparation:

1) Add all ingredients one by one or at the same time to your Mueller Austria juicer.
2) Process and stir.

Serving Suggestion: Add ice cubes if you want to serve your juice cold.

Tip: You can also use green apple for this recipe.

Cleansing Juice

Serves: 4
Preparation and Cooking Time: 10 minutes

Ingredients:

3 cucumbers, peeled
3 cups Romaine lettuce
2 apples
1 cup celery
1 lemon

Preparation:

1) Trim the ends of the Romaine lettuce and chop the remaining leaves and stems.
2) Run the ingredients to your Mueller Austria juicer.

Serving Suggestion: Chill before serving.

Tip: Use gala apples for this recipe.

Migraine Remedy Juice

Serves: 2
Preparation and Cooking Time: 10 minutes

Ingredients:

1 cup pineapple chunks
1 cup kale leaves
1 stalk celery
1 lemon
1/2 ginger

Preparation:

1) Run the ingredients through your Mueller Austria juicer.
2) Add water if you want your juice thinner.

Serving Suggestion: Garnish with lemon wedge.

Tip: You can also use spinach in place of kale.

Immunity Boosting Juice

Serves: 4
Preparation and Cooking Time: 5 minutes

Ingredients:

4 oranges
1 lemon
3 apples
1/2 ginger

Preparation:

1) Process all ingredients through your Mueller Austria juicer.
2) Serve with ice.

Serving Suggestion: Garnish with lemon wedge.

Tip: You can grate the ginger if you don't want to run it through juicer.

Breakfast Energizing Juice

Serves: 2
Preparation and Cooking Time: 10 minutes

Ingredients:

2 lemons
2 carrots
2 apples
2 beets

Preparation:

1) Chop all the ingredients.
2) Press through your Austria Mueller juicer.
3) Transfer to serving glasses.

Serving Suggestion: Chill before serving.

Tip: Do not peel the apples and carrots if you want your juice to be more nutritious.

Fruit Juices

Mango & Cherry Juice

Serves: 1
Preparation and Cooking Time: 15 minutes

Ingredients:

1 cup mango, sliced into cubes
3/4 cup water
1 cup frozen sweet cherries
1/2 cup water

Preparation:

1) Add mango to your Mueller Austria juicer.
2) Pour mango juice into a glass.
3) Stir in 3/4 cup water.
4) Process sweet cherries in the juicer.
5) Transfer to a glass and add 1/2 cup water.
6) Mix the two juices together.

Serving Suggestion: Garnish with cherry.

Tip: You can also use fresh cherry for this recipe.

Watermelon, Kiwi & Lime Juice

Serves: 1
Preparation and Cooking Time: 10 minutes

Ingredients:

2 kiwis
2 limes
2 cups watermelon

Preparation:

1)   Peel the kiwis and chop the watermelon.
2)   Press through your Mueller Austria juicer.

Serving Suggestion: Serve with ice.

Tip: Add a tablespoon of chia seeds to your juice.

Mango & Pineapple Juice

Serves: 1
Preparation and Cooking Time: 10 minutes

Ingredients:

2 cups mango, chopped
2 cups pineapple chunks
2 limes

Preparation:

1) Process mango cubes and pineapple chunks in your Mueller Austria juicer.
2) Slice the limes in half and run through the juicer.
3) Mix the juices.

Serving Suggestion: Chill in the refrigerator for 30 minutes.

Tip: You can also use orange or lime for this recipe if you don't have lime.

Strawberry & Apple Juice

Serves: 1
Preparation and Cooking Time: 5 minutes

Ingredients:

2 cups strawberries
2 apples

Preparation:

1) Slice the tops off the strawberries.
2) Juice the strawberries.
3) Slice the apples and run through the juicer.
4) Mix the juices and serve cold.

Serving Suggestion: Garnish with apple and strawberries slices.

Tip: You can also add other red or pink fruits to this recipe.

Lime, Watermelon & Cucumber Juice

Serves: 4
Preparation and Cooking Time: 10 minutes

Ingredients:

4 lb. watermelon
4 cucumbers
2 limes

Preparation:

1) Slice the watermelon and remove the seeds.
2) Press the watermelon through the Mueller Austria juicer.
3) Slice the cucumbers in half.
4) Run the cucumber through the juicer.
5) Juice the 2 limes.
6) Pour all the juices in serving glasses.

Serving Suggestion: Add ice, stir and serve.

Tip: You can also use lemon for this recipe.

Watermelon & Lychee Juice

Serves: 4
Preparation and Cooking Time: 10 minutes

Ingredients:

8 lychees
4 cups watermelon
1 lemon
10 mint leaves
1/2 cup sugar

Preparation:

1) Slice and pit the lychees.
2) Remove the seeds.
3) Press the lychees and watermelon through your Mueller Austria juicer.
4) Slice the lemon and process in the juicer.
5) Add juice to a pitcher.
6) In a blender, pulse mint leaves.
7) Stir this into the juice.
8) Add the sugar and mix.

Serving Suggestion: Serve with ice.

Tip: You can also use mint leaves as garnish.

Roasted Pineapple Juice

Serves: 4
Preparation and Cooking Time: 10 minutes

Ingredients:

4 cups pineapple chunks
1 lemon
1/2 teaspoon black pepper
1/2 teaspoon cumin powder
1/4 cup sugar

Preparation:

1) Roast pineapple in your oven or grill.
2) Press roasted pineapple through your Mueller Austria juicer.
3) Add juice to serving glasses.
4) Do the same with the lemon.
5) Stir in the rest of the ingredients.
Mix well.

Serving Suggestion: Garnish with mint leaves.

Tip: You can also use honey in place of sugar.

Lychee & Dill Juice

Serves: 1
Preparation and Cooking Time: 5 minutes

Ingredients:

8 lychees
1 lime
Dill sprigs

Preparation:

1) Peel the lychees and remove the seeds.
2) Press the lychees through the Mueller Austria juicer.
3) Slice the lime in half and extract juice.
4) Mix the two juices and stir in the dill sprigs.

Serving Suggestion: Serve with ice.

Tip: You can also use lemon in place of lime.

Mulberry, Orange & Grape Juice

Serves: 2
Preparation and Cooking Time: 15 minutes

Ingredients:

4 mulberries
1 orange
2 limes
2 cups grapes
2 tablespoons maple syrup

Preparation:

1) Process mulberries, orange, limes and grapes in your Mueller Austria juicer.
2) Stir in maple syrup.
3) Mix well and serve.

Serving Suggestion: Serve with crushed ice.

Tip: Squeeze mulberries with your hands before processing.

Fizzy Orange, Mango & Apple Juice

Serves: 2
Preparation and Cooking Time: 15 minutes

Ingredients:

1 lemon
2 oranges
2 mangoes
1 apple
1 cup soda water

Preparation:

1) Slice the lemon, oranges and mangoes in half.
2) Peel the apple and chop into smaller pieces.
3) Process all the fruits in your Mueller Austria juicer.
4) Stir in soda water and serve.

Serving Suggestion: Garnish with mint leaves.

Tip: You can also use sparkling lemonade in place of soda water.

Grape & Lychee Juice

Serves: 4
Preparation and Cooking Time: 15 minutes

Ingredients:

6 lychees
2 lemons
6 cups black grapes
2 tablespoons sugar

Preparation:

1) Peel the lychees and remove the seeds.
2) Slice the lemons in half.
3) Process lychees, lemons and black grapes in your Mueller Austria juicer.
4) Stir in sugar.
5) Chill in the refrigerator and serve.

Serving Suggestion: Garnish with lemon slices.

Tip: You can also use honey in place of sugar.

Plum Juice

Serves: 5
Preparation and Cooking Time: 10 minutes

Ingredients:

25 plums

Preparation:

1) Run the plums through your Mueller Austria juicer.
2) Transfer to serving glasses.
3) Chill before serving.

Serving Suggestion: Garnish with plum slice.

Tip: You can also slice the plums before juicing if you like.

Orange & Basil Juice

Serves: 2
Preparation and Cooking Time: 5 minutes

Ingredients:

4 oranges
10 fresh basil leaves

Preparation:

1) Slice the oranges in half.
2) Juice the oranges using your Mueller Austria juicer.
3) Stir in the fresh basil leaves.

Serving Suggestion: Serve with ice cubes.

Tip: Drizzle with honey.

Apple, Orange & Lemon Juice

Serves: 2
Preparation and Cooking Time: 15 minutes

Ingredients:

1 lemon
2 oranges
2 apples
2 cups water
1 teaspoon turmeric powder

Preparation:

1) Process lemon, oranges and apples through your Mueller Austria juicer.
2) Add juice to a glass with 2 cups of water.
3) Stir in turmeric powder.

Serving Suggestion: Garnish with orange or lemon wedge.

Tip: Reduce amount of ginger if you want your juice less spicy.

Watermelon Juice

Serves: 8
Preparation and Cooking Time: 15 minutes

Ingredients:

4 cups watermelon, sliced into cubes and seeded
4 slices lemon or lime
1/2 cup water
1/2 cup sugar

Preparation:

1) Process watermelon and lemon in your Mueller Austria juicer.
2) Transfer to a pitcher.
3) Pour in water.
4) Stir in sugar.

Serving Suggestion: Garnish with watermelon slice.

Tip: You can also freeze watermelon cubes before juicing.

Honeydew Juice

Serves: 4
Preparation and Cooking Time: 10 minutes

Ingredients:

1 honeydew melon
1 cup water
1 cup ice cubes
1 tablespoon honey
1 teaspoon white sugar

Preparation:

1) Slice the honeydew melon in half.
2) Remove the seeds.
3) Peel and then slice into smaller pieces.
4) Run through your Mueller Austria juicer.
5) Transfer to a glass pitcher.
6) Add water and ice cubes.
7) Stir in honey and sugar.

Serving Suggestion: Garnish with melon slice.

Tip: This recipe can also be used for other types of melon.

Cantaloupe Juice

Serves: 4
Preparation and Cooking Time: 10 minutes

Ingredients:

1 cantaloupe
1 cup milk
2 tablespoons white sugar

Preparation:

1) Slice the cantaloupe in half.
2) Remove the seeds.
3) Peel and slice into smaller chunks.
4) Press the cantaloupe pieces through your Mueller Austria juicer.
5) Stir in milk and white sugar.

Serving Suggestion: Garnish with cantaloupe slice.

Tip: To make this recipe vegan, replace milk with almond milk or coconut milk.

Minty Peach Juice

Serves: 1
Preparation and Cooking Time: 5 minutes

Ingredients:

1 apple
3 peaches
1 lime
5 fresh mint leaves

Preparation:

1) Juice the apple, peaches and lime using your Mueller Austria
    juicer.
2) Transfer to a serving glass.
3) Stir in the mint leaves.

Serving Suggestion: Garnish with peach slice.

Tip: You can also add a teaspoon brown sugar or a drizzle of honey
to sweeten your juice.

Fizzy Orange & Lemon Juice

Serves: 1
Preparation and Cooking Time: 5 minutes

Ingredients:

2 oranges
1 lemon
1 cup soda water

Preparation:

1) Process oranges and lemon in your Mueller Austria juicer.
2) Add soda water to the juice.

Serving Suggestion: Serve with ice.

Tip: You can also chill in the refrigerator first before serving.

Apple, Pear & Lemon Juice

Serves: 4
Preparation and Cooking Time: 10 minutes

Ingredients:

2 apples
2 pears
1 lemon
1-2 tablespoons white sugar

Preparation:

1) Slice apples and pears into smaller pieces.
2) Slice lemon in half.
3) Process apples, pears and lemon in your Mueller Austria juicer.
4) Stir in sugar and serve.

Serving Suggestion: Garnish with apple or lemon slice.

Tip: Adjust amount of sugar depending on your preference.

Banana Juice

Serves: 2
Preparation and Cooking Time: 5 minutes

Ingredients:

2 bananas
2 cups milk
1 tablespoon honey

Preparation:

1) Press bananas through your Mueller Austria juicer.
2) Add to serving glasses.
3) Pour in milk.
4) Stir in honey.

Serving Suggestion: Drizzle top with honey and serve.

Tip: Chop bananas before juicing.

Watermelon & Pineapple Juice

Serves: 12
Preparation and Cooking Time: 15 minutes

Ingredients:

1 lime
15 oz. pineapple chunks
1 watermelon, sliced and grated
3 cups water
1/2 cup coconut flakes
2 tablespoons white sugar

Preparation:

1) Process lime and pineapple chunks in your Austria Mueller juicer.
2) Place lime juice in a glass.
3) Stir in grated watermelon, water, coconut flakes and sugar.

Serving Suggestion: Sprinkle coconut flakes on top.

Tip: You can also use sweetened coconut flakes and skip sugar.

Pure Orange Juice

Serves: 1
Preparation and Cooking Time: 5 minutes

Ingredients:

4 oranges

Preparation:

1) Smack oranges on your kitchen counter.
2) Slice in half.
3) Press orange halves through your Mueller Austria juicer.

Serving Suggestion: Garnish with orange slice.

Tip: Feel free to add other fruits and vegetables as orange juice go well with many different ingredients.

Creamy Grapefruit & Strawberry Juice

Serves: 2
Preparation and Cooking Time: 15 minutes

Ingredients:

1 grapefruit
8 strawberries
2 bananas
2 tablespoons honey
8 oz. yogurt
1 cup ice cubes

Preparation:

1) Juice the grapefruit using your Mueller Austria juicer.
2) Add to serving glasses.
3) Do the same step for the strawberries and bananas.
4) Transfer juice to the glasses.
5) Stir in honey and yogurt.
6) Add ice cubes.

Serving Suggestion: Top with a dollop of yogurt.

Tip: Use plain low-fat yogurt.

Apple & Lemon Juice

Serves: 1
Preparation and Cooking Time: 5 minutes

Ingredients:

1 apple
1 lemon
1 tablespoon honey

Preparation:

1) Slice the apple into smaller pieces
2) Slice the lemon in half.
3) Juice the apple and lemon.
4) Stir in honey or drizzle on top.

Serving Suggestion: Garnish with lemon slice.

Tip: Use Fuji apples for this recipe.

Vegetable Juices

Veggie Juice with Yogurt

Serves: 4
Preparation and Cooking Time: 10 minutes

Ingredients:

1 lime
8 cups kale leaves
1 cup tomatoes, chopped
1 carrot, chopped
1 cucumber, chopped
1 stalk celery, chopped
1 tablespoon Greek yogurt
1 teaspoon ground cumin

Preparation:

1) Add all the ingredients except yogurt to your Mueller Austria juicer.
2) Process and mix.
3) Stir in yogurt and cumin.
4) Serve with ice.

Serving Suggestion: Garnish with lime slice.

Tip: Add water to thin the juice.

Aloe Vera & Veggie Juice

Serves: 2
Preparation and Cooking Time: 10 minutes

Ingredients:

1 cup kale
1 cup baby spinach
1 cup Swiss chard
1 cup aloe vera juice
2 tablespoons honey

Preparation:

1) Process kale, spinach and Swiss chard through your Mueller
    Austria juicer.
2) Add juice to 2 serving glasses.
3) Stir in aloe vera juice and honey.

Serving Suggestion: Garnish with kale leaves.

Tip: This recipe can also be made using a blender.

Cucumber & Carrot Juice

Serves: 2
Preparation and Cooking Time: 10 minutes

Ingredients:

2 carrots
1 cucumber
1 tablespoon fresh basil leaves, chopped

Preparation:

1) Process all the ingredients through your Mueller Austria juicer.
2) Serve immediately.

Serving Suggestion: Sprinkle juice with grated carrots before serving.

Tip: Chop the vegetables into smaller pieces before juicing.

Refreshing Cucumber Juice

Serves: 1
Preparation and Cooking Time: 5 minutes

Ingredients:

1 lime
2 cucumbers
1/2 cup water
1/4 cup white sugar

Preparation:

1) Process lime and cucumber in your Mueller Austria juicer.
2) Add water to the juice.
3) Stir in sugar.

Serving Suggestion: Garnish with chopped mint leaves.

Tip: You can also use lemon in place of lime. Add more water if you want your juice thinner.

Veggie Juice

Serves: 2
Preparation and Cooking Time: 15 minutes

Ingredients:

1 cup Romaine lettuce, chopped
1/4 cup chives, chopped
1/4 jalapeño pepper, seeded
2 stalks celery
1 red bell pepper, sliced into strips
2 tomatoes, sliced
1 carrot, peeled

Preparation:

1) Press lettuce and chives through your Mueller Austria juicer.
2) Next, run the jalapeño pepper, celery and red bell pepper to be followed by the tomatoes and carrot.

Serving Suggestion: Chill in the refrigerator before serving.

Tip: You can also choose not to peel your carrots.

Combination Juices

Kale, Green Apple & Ginger Lemonade

Serves: 2
Preparation and Cooking Time: 10 minutes

Ingredients:

2 cups kale
1 green apple, sliced
1 cup cilantro
1 clove garlic, peeled
1 ginger
1 cucumber
1 lemon

Preparation:

1) Run the ingredients through your Mueller Austria juicer.
2) Serve immediately.

Serving Suggestion: Garnish with lemon wedge.

Tip: Chop the vegetables into smaller pieces before running through the juicer.

Green Juice

Serves: 4 to 6
Preparation and Cooking Time: 15 minutes

Ingredients:

1 lemon
2 oranges
2 green apples
1 cup Swiss chard
1 cup kale leaves
1 cup spinach
1 cucumber
6 stalks celery
1 ginger
1 cup parsley
1/2 gallon water
1 teaspoon turmeric powder
1/2 teaspoon spirulina powder

Preparation:

1) Process lemon, oranges and green apples through your Mueller
    Austria juicer.
2) Do the same step for the leafy greens, cucumber, celery, ginger
    and parsley.
3) Add juices to water.
4) Stir in turmeric powder and spirulina powder.

Serving Suggestion: Serve with ice.

Tip: Chill in the refrigerator. Consume within the day.

Apple & Carrot Juice

Serves: 6
Preparation and Cooking Time: 10 minutes

Ingredients:

15 oz. pineapple chunks
3 carrots
1 apple, sliced into wedges
1 beet
2 stalks celery
2 teaspoons ginger, minced
1 teaspoon white sugar

Preparation:

1) Juice the pineapple, carrots, apples, beet, celery and ginger through your Mueller Austria juicer.
2) Transfer to serving glasses.
3) Stir in white sugar.

Serving Suggestion: Garnish with apple or pineapple slice.

Tip: Trim the ends of carrots before processing through the juicer.

Green Lemonade

Serves: 1
Preparation and Cooking Time: 10 minutes

Ingredients:

2 cups Romaine lettuce
1 cup kale
2 apples
1 lemon
1 ginger, grated

Preparation:

1) Chop Romaine lettuce and kale.
2) Process through your Mueller Austria juicer.
3) Juice apples and lemon.
4) Mix juices together in a glass pitcher.
5) Stir in grated ginger.

Serving Suggestion: Serve with ice or chill in the refrigerator for 30 minutes before serving.

Tip: You can also juice ginger with the lemon and apples if you like.

Tomato Juice

Serves: 6
Preparation and Cooking Time: 10 minutes

Ingredients:

4 cups tomatoes
2 cups water
1 lemon
6 oz. tomato paste
2 tablespoons white sugar

Preparation:

1) Chop tomatoes into smaller pieces.
2) Run chopped tomatoes through your Austria Mueller juicer.
3) Transfer to a glass pitcher.
4) Juice the lemon.
5) Add lemon juice to the pitcher.
6) Stir tomato paste and sugar.

Serving Suggestion: Garnish with tomato slices.

Tip: You can add more water if you like your juice thinner.

Apple, Spinach & Grapefruit Juice

Serves: 2
Preparation and Cooking Time: 15 minutes

Ingredients:

2 green apples, sliced
1-1/2 cups spinach
1 grapefruit, peeled and trimmed
2 stalks celery
1 ginger

Preparation:

1) Process the ingredients through your Mueller Austria juicer in this order: apples, spinach, grapefruit, celery and ginger.
2) Serve immediately.

Serving Suggestion: Serve with ice.

Tip: You can also use spinach for this recipe.

Cucumber & Strawberry Juice

Serves: 2
Preparation and Cooking Time: 15 minutes

Ingredients:

6 strawberries, sliced
1 cucumber, sliced
1 apple, sliced
2 carrots

Preparation:

1)   Process all the ingredients through your Mueller Austria juicer.

Serving Suggestion: Sprinkle with grated apple or carrots on top before serving.

Tip: You can also use frozen strawberries for this recipe.

Blueberry Power Juice

Serves: 2
Preparation and Cooking Time: 15 minutes

Ingredients:

2 cups blueberries
1 apple, sliced
1 cucumber, sliced into cubes
1 cup red cabbage

Preparation:

1) Run the blueberries, apple, cucumber and cabbage through your Mueller Austria juicer.

Serving Suggestion: Garnish with chopped blueberries.

Tip: You can also add other berries into this recipe.

Green Apple, Cucumber & Lemon Juice

Serves: 1
Preparation and Cooking Time: 10 minutes

Ingredients:

2 green apples
1 cucumber
1 lemon
1/2 cup cold water

Preparation:

1) Slice green apples into wedges.
2) Slice cucumber and lemon in half.
3) Process green apple, cucumber and lemon in your Mueller
   Austria juicer.
4) Add juice to a serving glass.
5) Stir in cold water.

Serving Suggestion: Garnish with cucumber or lemon slice.

Tip: Sweeten with honey or maple syrup.

Orange, Carrot & Cucumber Juice

Serves: 4
Preparation and Cooking Time: 10 minutes

Ingredients:

1/2 lemon
1 orange
1 cucumber
2 carrots
1/2 cup cold water
1/4 cup white sugar

Preparation:

1) Process lemon through your Mueller Austria juicer.
2) Place freshly squeezed lemon juice in a glass.
3) Press orange, cucumber and carrots to your juicer.
4) Add juice to the glass.
5) Stir in cold water and white sugar.

Serving Suggestion: Add ice cubes and serve.

Tip: You can replace white sugar with honey or maple syrup.

Pear, Cucumber & Celery Juice

Serves: 2
Preparation and Cooking Time: 1 hour and 10 minutes

Ingredients:

1 pear
1 cucumber
2 stalks celery

Preparation:

1) Slice the pear into smaller pieces.
2) Slice the cucumber in half.
3) Chop the celery.
4) Run all ingredients through your Mueller Austria juicer.
5) Chill for 1 hour in the refrigerator and serve.

Serving Suggestion: Garnish with cucumber slice.

Tip: You can also add ice cubes so you can serve the juice right away.

Ginger & Apple Juice

Serves: 2
Preparation and Cooking Time: 10 minutes

Ingredients:

1/4 lemon
2 apples
5 carrots
1 ginger

Preparation:

1) Process lemon through your Mueller Austria juicer.
2) Transfer lemon juice to 2 serving glasses.
3) Repeat the steps with the apple, carrots and ginger.
4) Add these to the glasses.
5) Stir and serve.

Serving Suggestion: Garnish with lemon wedge or apple slice.

Tip: There is no need to peel the carrots.

Pineapple, Kale & Banana Juice

Serves: 1
Preparation and Cooking Time: 10 minutes

Ingredients:

1 cup pineapple chunks
4 kale leaves
1 banana

Preparation:

1) Press ingredients through the Mueller Austria juicer.
2) Serve immediately.

Serving Suggestion: Drizzle with honey before serving.

Tip: Add crushed ice if you want your juice cold.

Apple & Kale Juice

Serves: 1
Preparation and Cooking Time: 5 minutes

Ingredients:

2 apples
5 kale leaves

Preparation:

1) Slice apples into wedges.
2) Process in your Mueller Austria juicer.
3) Transfer to a serving glass.
4) Repeat step with the kale leaves.
5) Add to the glass and mix.

Serving Suggestion: Drizzle with honey before serving.

Tip: Use tart apples for this recipe.

Cucumber & Cantaloupe Juice

Serves: 4
Preparation and Cooking Time: 10 minutes

Ingredients:

1/2 cantaloupe
1 cucumber
1 lemon
2 stalks celery
1/4 cup mint leaves

Preparation:

1) Slice cantaloupe into smaller pieces without peeling.
2) Remove seeds.
3) Press through the Mueller Austria juicer.
4) Slice cucumber and lemon in half.
5) Process in the juicer.
6) Do the same step for the celery.
7) Add all the juices in serving glasses.
8) Stir in mint leaves.

Serving Suggestion: Chill in the refrigerator or add ice before serving.

Tip: Make sure you use ripe cantaloupe for this recipe.

Parsley & Apple Lemonade

Serves: 2
Preparation and Cooking Time: 5 minutes

Ingredients:

1/4 cup parsley
2 apples
2 lemons
1 cup spinach leaves

Preparation:

1) Chop the vegetables.
2) Slice apples and lemons in half.
3) Process all the ingredients in Mueller Austria juicer.
4) Add to serving glasses and serve.

Serving Suggestion: Add ice before serving.

Tip: This juice is best consumed within 15 minutes but you can also refrigerate for up to 1 day.

Pineapple & Celery Juice

Serves: 2
Preparation and Cooking Time: 5 minutes

Ingredients:

1 apple
4 kale leaves
2 cups pineapple chunks
2 stalks celery

Preparation:

1) Slice apples into smaller pieces.
2) Chop kale leaves.
3) Add all the ingredients to your Mueller Austria juicer and process.

Serving Suggestion: Garnish with pineapple wedge.

Tip: You can use either fresh or frozen pineapple chunks for this recipe.

Apple & Celery Juice

Serves: 2
Preparation and Cooking Time: 10 minutes

Ingredients:

2 apples
4 stalks celery
1 cup pineapple chunks
1 ginger

Preparation:

1) Slice the apples in half.
2) Chop celery and mince ginger.
3) Press ingredients through your Mueller Austria juicer.
4) Pour juices into serving glasses.

Serving Suggestion: Sprinkle with powdered sugar on top before serving.

Tip: You can skip the ginger if you want less spice in your juice.

Beet, Carrot & Apple Juice

Serves: 2
Preparation and Cooking Time: 5 minutes

Ingredients:

1 lemon
1 apple
1 beet
2 carrots

Preparation:

1) Slice lemon and apple in half.
2) Chop beet and carrots.
3) Run all the ingredients through your Mueller Austria juicer.

Serving Suggestion: Chill the juice before serving.

Tip: Include beet greens if possible to increase nutritional content.

Spicy Carrot & Ginger Juice

Serves: 2
Preparation and Cooking Time: 10 minutes

Ingredients:

6 carrots
1 orange
1 ginger
1 teaspoon turmeric powder
1/4 teaspoon cayenne pepper

Preparation:

1) Slice the carrots and orange in half.
2) Process these and the ginger in the Mueller Austria juicer.
3) Stir in the turmeric powder and cayenne pepper.

Serving Suggestion: Add ice to your juice before serving.

Tip: Add more cayenne pepper if you like your juice spicier.

Grapefruit & Ginger Juice

Serves: 4
Preparation and Cooking Time: 10 minutes

Ingredients:

2 grapefruits
1 ginger
3 sprigs mint

Preparation:

1) Slice grapefruits into smaller pieces.
2) Process through your Mueller Austria juicer.
3) Add ginger and press through the juicer.
4) Transfer to serving glasses.
5) Stir in mint.

Serving Suggestion: Garnish with mint leaves.

Tip: You can also sweeten this juice with honey and maple syrup.

Pear, Celery & Lemon Juice

Serves: 1
Preparation and Cooking Time: 5 minutes

Ingredients:

2 pears
2 lemons
3 stalks celery

Preparation:

1) Peel the pears and remove the core.
2) Slice the lemons in half.
3) Press pears, lemons and celery through your Mueller Austria juicer.

Serving Suggestion: Add crushed ice to your juice before serving.

Tip: You can also use apple if you don't have pears.

Pear, Sweet Potato & Cinnamon Juice

Serves: 1
Preparation and Cooking Time: 5 minutes

Ingredients:

3 sweet potatoes
1 pear
1/4 teaspoon ground cinnamon

Preparation:

1) Peel the sweet potatoes and slice in half.
2) Press through the Mueller Austria juicer.
3) Add the pear to the juicer.
4) Mix the juices.
5) Stir in the ground cinnamon.

Serving Suggestion: Chill in the refrigerator for 30 minutes before serving.

Tip: You can also choose not to peel the sweet potatoes if you want to add more fiber to your juice.

Kale & Carrot Juice

Serves: 2
Preparation and Cooking Time: 5 minutes

Ingredients:

2 apples
2 carrots
1 1/2 lb. kale

Preparation:

1) Peel the carrots.
2) Slice the apples in half.
3) Pass the apples, carrots and kale through your Mueller Austria juicer.
4) Pour the juice into serving glasses.

Serving Suggestion: Sprinkle with powdered sugar on top.

Tip: Use Honeycrisp apples for this recipe.

Sweet Potato & Beet Juice

Serves: 2
Preparation and Cooking Time: 10 minutes

Ingredients:

1 orange
1 lime
2 apples
1 sweet potato
1/4 teaspoon ground cinnamon

Preparation:

1) Slice orange and lime in half.
2) Chop apples and sweet potatoes.
3) Process all these in your Mueller Austria juicer.
4) Stir in ground cinnamon and serve.

Serving Suggestion: Sprinkle ground cinnamon on top before serving.

Tip: You can also choose not to peel the sweet potato.

Orange & Carrot Juice

Serves: 4
Preparation and Cooking Time: 10 minutes

Ingredients:

6 carrots
2 apples
3 oranges
Honey

Preparation:

1) Peel the carrots and slice in half.
2) Slice apples and oranges in half.
3) Run the ingredients through your Mueller Austria juicer.
4) Sweeten your juice with honey.

Serving Suggestion: Garnish with orange slice.

Tip: You can also use sugar or maple syrup to sweeten the juice.

Apple, Carrot & Berry Juice

Serves: 4
Preparation and Cooking Time: 15 minutes

Ingredients:

8 carrots
3 apples
1 cup strawberries
1 cup blueberries

Preparation:

1) Peel the carrots and apples.
2) Press these through your Mueller Austria juicer.
3) Add the berries to your juicer.
4) Mix the juices together and chill before serving.

Serving Suggestion: Top with chopped strawberry and serve.

Tip: You can add other types of berries to this recipe.

Sweet Potato, Apple, Celery & Orange Juice

Categories:
Preparation and Cooking Time: 10 minutes

Ingredients:

2 apples
2 pears
3 stalks celery
1 orange
1 sweet potato

Preparation:

1) Peel the apples and pears, and then slice in half.
2) Chop the celery.
3) Slice the orange in half.
4) Process all ingredients using your Mueller Austria juicer.
5) Mix the juice and serve immediately.

Serving Suggestion: Garnish with pear wedge.

Tip: Replace orange with lemon if you want your juice more sour.

Spinach, Lemon & Kale Juice

Categories:
Preparation and Cooking Time: 10 minutes

Ingredients:

4 apples
2 lemons
3 stalks celery
4 cups spinach
2 cups kale

Preparation:

1) Slice the apples and lemons in half.
2) Chop the veggies in smaller pieces.
3) Press all the ingredients through your Mueller Austria juicer.
4) Mix all.

Serving Suggestion: Insert a celery stalk in your juice and serve.

Tip: Sweeten with honey or maple syrup.

Apple, Beets & Ginger Juice

Categories:
Preparation and Cooking Time: 15 minutes

Ingredients:

8 carrots
2 apples
2 beets
1/2 ginger
1 lemon

Preparation:

1) Peel the carrots and apples.
2) Slice into smaller pieces.
3) Chop the beets and ginger.
4) Slice the lemon in half.
5) Process all ingredients through your Mueller Austria juicer.
6) Mix well.

Serving Suggestion: Chill in the refrigerator for 30 minutes before serving.

Tip: You can also juice the carrots with the peel.

Peach, Carrot & Apple Juice

Categories:
Preparation and Cooking Time: 10 minutes

Ingredients:

2 apples
10 carrots
1 lemon
1 orange
2 peaches

Preparation:

1) Peel the apples and carrots.
2) Slice the lemon and orange in half.
3) Press all the ingredients through your Mueller Austria juicer.
4) Mix well.

Serving Suggestion: Serve with ice.

Tip: Drizzle with honey or maple syrup if you want your juice
sweeter.

Kiwi, Cucumber & Celery Juice

Categories:
Preparation and Cooking Time: 10 minutes

Ingredients:

4 kiwis
2 cucumbers
1/2 ginger
1 stalk celery

Preparation:

1) Peel the kiwis, cucumber and ginger.
2) Chop into smaller pieces.
3) Chill the vegetables in the refrigerator for 1 hour.
4) Press the vegetables through the Mueller Austria juicer.
5) Pour the juice into serving glasses.

Serving Suggestion: Garnish with sprouts.

Tip: Use extra celery stalk as stirrer.

Pineapple & Kale Juice

Categories:
Preparation and Cooking Time: 10 minutes

Ingredients:

2 cups pineapple chunks
1 stalk celery
1 cup spinach leaves
4 kale leaves
1 orange
1 lime

Preparation:

1) Process pineapple chunks in your Mueller Austria juicer.
2) Chop the celery, spinach and kale leaves.
3) Add to the juicer and process.
4) Slice the orange and lime in half.
5) Do the same step.
6) Mix all the juices.

Serving Suggestion: Serve with crushed ice.

Tip: Use an extra celery stalk as stirrer.

Orange, Cucumber & Carrot Juice

Categories:
Preparation and Cooking Time: 10 minutes

Ingredients:

6 carrots
1 cucumber
1 orange
1 ginger
1 tablespoon basil leaves

Preparation:

1) Process all the ingredients except the basil leaves through your Mueller Austria juicer.
2) Chop the basil leaves in small pieces and add to the juice.

Serving Suggestion: Chill in the refrigerator for 30 minutes before serving.

Tip: You can also use mint leaves in place of basil.

Fruit & Veggie Loaded Juice

Categories:
Preparation and Cooking Time: 15 minutes

Ingredients:

1 carrot
1 cucumber
1 orange
1 lemon
1 ginger
4 celery stalks
2 apples
1 cup strawberry

Preparation:

1)   Slice the carrot, cucumber, orange and lemon in half.
2)   Chop the ginger and celery stalks.
3)   Slice the apples and strawberries into smaller pieces.
4)   Process all these through your Mueller Austria juicer.
5)   Mix well.
6)   Chill before serving.

Serving Suggestion: Garnish with lemon wedges.

Tip: Use curly kale for this recipe.

Cucumber, Watermelon & Strawberry Juice

Categories:
Preparation and Cooking Time: 1 hour and 15 minutes

Ingredients:

10 strawberries
4 cups watermelon
1 cucumber

Preparation:

1) Slice the watermelon into smaller cubes.
2) Remove the watermelon rind.
3) Press through your Mueller Austria juicer.
4) Refrigerate for 1 hour before serving.

Serving Suggestion: Garnish with watermelon slice.

Tip: Freeze watermelon before juicing.

Autumn Juice

Categories:
Preparation and Cooking Time: 10 minutes

Ingredients:

6 apples
2 oranges
4 cups Swiss chard
2 stalks celery

Preparation:

1) Peel oranges and slice in half.
2) Chop the remaining ingredients.
3) Add all ingredients to your Mueller Austria juicer.

Serving Suggestion: Garnish with apple slice.

Tip: Strain the juice if you want smoother texture.

Conclusion

Individuals have a unique microbiota that influences a large aspect of their health.

The enzymatic fluid from raw-juiced produce kick starts the production of healthy bacteria in the gut that will strengthen the body's immunity and improve bodily functions.

Juicing will help the gut soak up the vitamins and minerals faster, making it a great option for people with malabsorption and digestive issues.

Juicing allows us to increase our intake of essential nourishment found in raw produce.

Drinking green juice, along with a balanced diet, is a superb way to maintain a healthy mind and body.

The Mueller Austria's juicer is perfect for anyone planning to start juicing as it is a compact, user-friendly, and affordable juicer. It also has considerable great reviews online.

It is sturdy enough to handle most produce while looking very stylish and modern. On top of that, its powerful motor is highly capable of churning out juice within seconds.

If you are looking for a high-speed juice extractor that is also a bang for your buck, then the Mueller Austria's juicer is your best option.

www.ingramcontent.com/pod-product-compliance
Lightning Source LLC
Chambersburg PA
CBHW081946160726
47999CB00008B/2535